CELEBRATING THE FAMILY NAME OF PALMER

Celebrating the Family Name of Palmer

Walter the Educator

Silent King Books
a WhichHead Entertainment Imprint

Copyright © 2024 by Walter the Educator

All rights reserved. No part of this book may be reproduced in any manner whatsoever without written permission except in the case of brief quotations embodied in critical articles and reviews.

First Printing, 2024

Disclaimer

This book is a literary work; the story is not about specific persons, locations, situations, and/or circumstances unless mentioned in a historical context. Any resemblance to real persons, locations, situations, and/or circumstances is coincidental. This book is for entertainment and informational purposes only. The author and publisher offer this information without warranties expressed or implied. No matter the grounds, neither the author nor the publisher will be accountable for any losses, injuries, or other damages caused by the reader's use of this book. The use of this book acknowledges an understanding and acceptance of this disclaimer.

Celebrating the Family Name of Palmer is a memory book that belongs to the Celebrating Family Name Book Series by Walter the Educator. Collect them all and more books at WaltertheEducator.com

USE THE EXTRA SPACE TO DOCUMENT YOUR FAMILY MEMORIES THROUGHOUT THE YEARS

PALMER

Upon the earth where roots run deep,

Celebrating the Family Name of
Palmer

Where ancient winds in whispers sweep,

The name of Palmer stands in grace,

A banner held through time and space.

From lands where pilgrims used to roam,

To hearths that hold the light of home,

Each footstep echoes through the years,

A tapestry of hopes and fears.

The palmers once, with staffs in hand,

Traversed the roads of foreign lands,

But in their hearts, a map was drawn,

To guide them back before the dawn.

The name is more than soil and seed,

It is a call, a whispered creed.

A bridge of blood, of faith, of might,

That bends but never breaks to light.

Celebrating the Family Name of
Palmer

Through valleys low and mountains high,

The Palmers raised their heads to sky,

In rain or shine, they forged ahead,

A fire within, by vision led.

Beneath the oaks, beneath the pines,

The name endures, the bloodline shines.

In hands that worked, in dreams that dared,

In eyes that loved, in hearts that cared.

Through wars and peace, through joy and tears,

The Palmer name survived the years.

It's found in laughter, found in song,

It's found where family makes us strong.

Like leaves that fall and bloom again,

So does the legacy remain,

Not just in stone, not just in land,

But in the love of those who stand.

For every branch that stretches wide,

Another story springs with pride.

The Palmer tree grows tall and free,

Celebrating the Family Name of
Palmer

Its roots entwined with destiny.

In every corner, every age,

They've written lines on history's page.

With every hand that sowed or built,

The Palmer name erased no guilt.

ABOUT THE CREATOR

Walter the Educator is one of the pseudonyms for Walter Anderson. Formally educated in Chemistry, Business, and Education, he is an educator, an author, a diverse entrepreneur, and he is the son of a disabled war veteran. "Walter the Educator" shares his time between educating and creating. He holds interests and owns several creative projects that entertain, enlighten, enhance, and educate, hoping to inspire and motivate you. Follow, find new works, and stay up to date with Walter the Educator™

at WaltertheEducator.com

www.ingramcontent.com/pod-product-compliance
Lightning Source LLC
LaVergne TN
LVHW012052070526
838201LV00082B/3919